WHY DO I
WEAR A MASK?

BY Madeline Tyler

BookLife
PUBLISHING

©2021
BookLife Publishing Ltd.
King's Lynn
Norfolk PE30 4LS

All rights reserved.
Printed in Malta.

A catalogue record for
this book is available from
the British Library.

ISBN: 978-1-83927-695-8

Written by:
Madeline Tyler

Edited by:
John Wood

Designed by:
Danielle Rippengill

Image Credits

All images are courtesy of Shutterstock.com, unless otherwise specified. With thanks to Getty Images, Thinkstock Photo and iStockphoto. Front Cover & 1 – PPBR, julio chaniago, Nadzin, Dmitry Natashin. Images used on every page – Nadzin, Dmitry Natashin. 4 – Andy Frith. 5 – Iconic Bestiary. 6 – Glinskaja Olga, yusufdemirci. 7&8 – Iconic Bestiary. 9 – PPBR, julio chaniago. 10–13 – Iconic Bestiary. 13 – jehsomwang. 14–23 – Iconic Bestiary. 23 – Pemimpi.

CONTENTS

Words that look like **this** can be found in the glossary on page 24.

What Are Germs?

Germs are tiny things that are too small to see. Most germs do not hurt us, but some germs can make us ill if they get into our bodies.

Germs can live on our skin and on the **surfaces** of things.

They can also be found
in the air around us, and
the air we breathe in.

5

HOW DO Germs Spread?

You can't see when something is covered in germs because they are so small. When you touch things, your hands can **spread** germs from one thing to another.

Wash your hands a lot to get rid of any germs that could be on them.

Germs from someone's nose and mouth can end up in the air by breathing, coughing or sneezing. These germs can land on things or be breathed in by someone else.

If somebody is ill, the germs they pass on could make other people ill.

Why Do We Wear Masks?

Wearing a mask or face covering can help to stop germs spreading. The mask catches germs from your nose and mouth and stops them from getting into the air.

A face covering is any **material** that covers your nose and mouth.

Masks and face coverings help to **protect** you and other people from getting ill. They stop germs from getting into the air, which means nobody can breathe them in.

This helps to stop <u>diseases</u> spreading.

Different Types of Face Coverings

There are lots of different types of face coverings.
Here are a few.

Reusable
Cloth Mask

Face
Shield

Some masks are better than others at protecting you from germs.

Scarf

Bandana

Medical mask

Gaiter

How to
Wear a mask

When you wear a mask or face covering, it should always cover your nose, your mouth and your chin. There shouldn't be any gaps around your mask.

When people wear a mask properly, they spread fewer germs.

✔️

❌

Always wash your hands before you put a mask or face covering on.

Try not to touch your mask when you're wearing it. This keeps it clean.

Wash your hands after you take off your mask.

Wrong Ways to Wear a Mask

You should always make sure you wear a mask in the right way.
Here are some wrong ways that people might wear masks.

Wearing a mask in the wrong way will not protect you or other people. Germs will spread, and so might diseases.

When to Wear a mask

Different people wear masks at different times and for different reasons.

Some people wear masks on buses, trains and planes.

Some people wear masks when they go shopping or are near lots of other people.

Some people wear masks whenever they are ill. This helps to protect other people from getting ill.

Who Doesn't Wear a Mask?

Lots of people don't wear masks. Some people are told by a doctor that they do not need to wear a mask.

Many children don't wear masks until they are around 12 years old.

Some **disabled people** find it difficult to put a mask on or take one off so they may not wear one.

Some people find it difficult to hear. These people might **lip read**. Someone who lip reads may ask anyone helping them not to wear a mask so that they can understand them.

makeshift masks

It's easy to make your own reusable mask at home.

How to make your mask

You will need:

- A piece of material or a handkerchief around 50 centimetres long and 50 centimetres wide
- 1 coffee filter
- 2 elastic bands

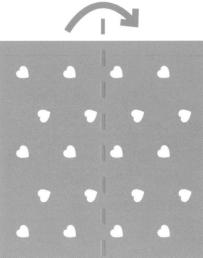

1. Fold your material in half.

2. Place the coffee filter in the middle of your rectangle.

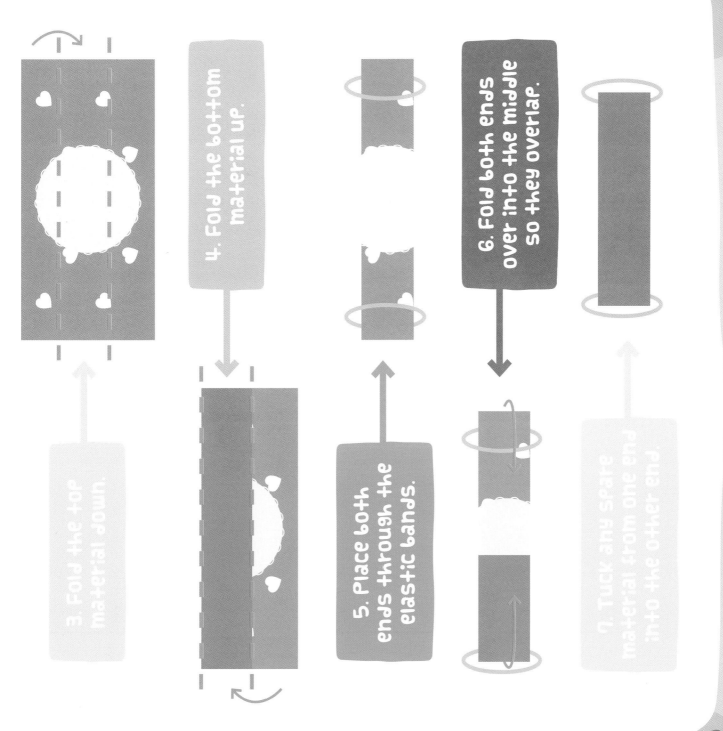

3. Fold the top material down.

4. Fold the bottom material up.

5. Place both ends through the elastic bands.

6. Fold both ends over into the middle so they overlap.

7. Tuck any spare material from one end into the other end.

How to Wear Your Mask

1. Put the elastic bands over your ears.

2. Pull the fabric up over your nose.

3. Pull the lower fabric down to cover your chin.

Caring for your mask

Different masks and face coverings need to be cared for in different ways.

Disposable masks can only be worn once. Cut the loops and put it in a bin.

Reusable masks need to be washed after every time you wear them.

Glossary

disabled people — people who find it difficult to do some or many day-to-day activities because of how a part of their body or mind wor

diseases — illnesses that cause harm to the health of a person

disposable — made to be thrown away after using

lip read — to understand what a person is saying by only looking at their lips

material — what an object is made from, such as fabric or cloth

medical — used by doctors and nurses in hospitals

protect — keep something safe and stop it from coming to harm

reusable — can be used more than once

spread — to move to other areas

surfaces — the outside or top layer of things

Index